one pot
recipes

SIMPLE RECIPES FOR
STUNNING MEALS

LINDA DOESER

This is a Parragon Publishing Book
First published in 2004

Parragon Publishing
Queen Street House
4 Queen Street
Bath BA1 1HE, UK

Created and produced by The Bridgewater Book Company Ltd.

ISBN: 1-40543-163-6

Printed in China

NOTE

*This book uses imperial, metric, and US cup measurements. Follow the same units of
measurement throughout; do not mix imperial and metric. All spoon measurements
are level: teaspoons are assumed to be 5 ml and tablespoons are assumed to be 15 ml.
Unless otherwise stated, milk is assumed to be whole, eggs and individual vegetables
such as potatoes are medium, and pepper is freshly ground black pepper.*

*Ovens should be preheated to the specified temperature. If using a fan-assisted oven,
check the manufacturer's instructions for adjusting the time and temperature.*

*Recipes using raw or very lightly cooked eggs should be avoided by infants, the elderly,
pregnant women, convalescents, and anyone suffering from an illness. Pregnant and
breastfeeding women are advised to avoid eating peanuts and peanut products.*

Contents

Introduction

Preparing food at home can give you a great sense of satisfaction, but it can seem something of a chore, and clearing up afterward is often very tedious. Running a household, holding down a job, and feeding the family can be difficult to balance, and with that hectic lifestyle, it is all too tempting to resort to unhealthy and expensive takeouts and convenience foods.

are also ideal complete meals for freezing. Finally, you can save even more time by keeping your pantry stocked up. The one-pot recipes in this book include everything from traditional stews, soups, and bakes to more unusual dishes from the Middle East, Mexico, and the Mediterranean and delicious desserts—dishes for every occasion.

One-pot meals are the ideal time-saving solution: they are more economical and healthier alternatives to convenience foods and are almost as easy, so why not try them for parties, Sunday lunches, or family suppers? They make weekdays easier, create less dishwashing, and involve less preparation than many other dishes, and they

Less Mess

One-pot dishes are the ideal way of cutting down on the dishwashing. They eliminate the need for extra pans or skillets and several serving dishes—most of these recipes can be served straight from the cooking pot. Try to find an attractive set of casseroles that you can serve from at the table, whether cooking for the family or entertaining guests. Look for ones that are freezer-proof as well as ovenproof to save even more time and dishwashing.

Freezing for the Future

Many one-pot meals can be frozen for future use: double the ingredients, and, when cooked, leave half to cool. Freeze in a rigid container, freezerproof casserole, or freezer bag for up to three months. To thaw, remove from the freezer 12 hours before you want your meal, leave at room temperature, then heat in the microwave.

experiment by using ingredients buried at the back of the pantry. Most of us keep the basics, such as pasta, rice, and canned tomatoes, but next time you go shopping, spend some time in the canned food aisle and select a few more unusual ingredients to try in the future.

Stocking the Pantry

Although you can't beat the unique flavor and texture of fresh vegetables, there are alternatives that can make a delicious last-minute lunch or supper. Keep your pantry well stocked to prevent a last-minute rush to the supermarket. Ingredients in jars or cans save on preparation time too—most items can be bought chopped, peeled, or flavored at little or no extra cost. Improvise by using chickpeas when the recipe calls for kidney beans, and for new dishes

Equipment

Investing in good quality equipment is important. Poor quality pans and dishes do not cook food evenly, and are difficult to clean. The most important pans for one-pot cooking are lidded casserole dishes, pans, and skillets. When making casseroles and pot roasts, you need to select a dish large enough to give the ingredients room to cook, but not so much room that they dry out.

If you are planning to cook lots of casseroles and stews, an ovenproof casserole is a good option. A solid, heavy-bottom casserole can be expensive, but is worth the cost, as the food will be evenly cooked and flavorsome. These pots can be used on the stove and in the oven. Cast-iron casseroles are best of all, but remember that they are very heavy when full.

Woks, skillets, and karahis (the Indian version of a wok) are also used for one-pot dishes, especially for stir-frying. Roasting pans are ideal for cooking one-pot roasts, with the vegetables sizzling in the juices from the meat. You may prefer a nonstick lining, but whatever type you choose, make sure that it is solid and large, and that the sides are of an adequate height, or you may find that the cooking juices drip dangerously over the rim.

You should think about the dishes you plan to cook and, therefore, the type of pan you will find most useful. If you cook on an electric stove with a flat surface, select a wok with a flat bottom, for example. A thick, solid bottom is important to allow even distribution of heat. If the manufacturer's instructions advise you to season a pan before you use it, do so, because this both improves the quality of cooking and extends the lifespan of the pan.

You will probably already have most of the other necessary utensils, but there may be some,

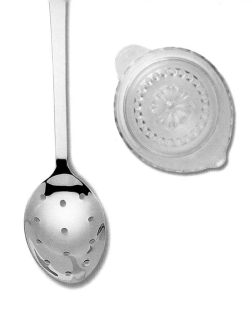

such as a zester, that you need to buy. Zesters are inexpensive and readily available. Using a zester is far easier than trying to grate lemon or orange rind then scrape it from the inside of the grater— and easier to clean, too. Cutting boards are an essential item and will last a long time. Whether you prefer wood or plastic, select a good, solid board that will not slip easily. Remember to use a separate board for raw meat. It is now thought that you should avoid cleaning utensils with antibacterial products, because various strains of bacteria can become completely resistant. Hot, soapy water is perfectly adequate for all pans and utensils; soak them first if there is any food stuck on the bottom.

Measuring cups and spoons with clear, easy-to-read numbers are essential. Although you can estimate amounts with many casseroles and stews, some dishes require exact measurements. Make sure you have a full set of imperial or metric measuring equipment and, when following the recipes, remember to stick to one or the other: the two systems are not interchangeable.

Other tools you will need include a slotted spoon for draining and serving—very valuable in one-pot cooking when, for instance, you may need to remove the meat ahead of the sauce. Try to find a good set of plastic utensils for nonstick surfaces or stainless steel for other dishes—these will last for years. A pestle and mortar is another necessity if you want to use freshly ground spices; these will always add a better flavor and color than ready-ground ones.

Good quality, sharp knives make the cook's life a lot easier, saving time and increasing safety

in the kitchen. You should also buy a knife sharpener and sharpen your knives regularly— using blunt knives is dangerous. A carving knife is ideal for carving pot roasts and other joints of meat. One large chopping knife with a heavy blade is useful for a multitude of purposes, but you may find a range of different sized knives suits you. A paring knife, being smaller and lighter, is perfect for trimming, peeling, and chopping small vegetables.

Nowadays, there are ways to speed up preparation. For a real time-saver, invest in a food processor—a good quality one will last for a long time. Alternatively, most supermarkets now stock washed, peeled, and chopped raw vegetables, as well as their range of frozen and canned goods, which are a boon when you are short of time for preparing a meal. Canned foods never taste as good as raw ingredients and often have little texture and color, but some, such as plum tomatoes and beans, are invaluable.

Meat

& Fish

Cock-a-Leekie

Two for the price of one—serve the soup separately as a first course and the meat and vegetables as a main course. Alternatively, for a really chunky dish, ladle the whole thing into large soup plates.

serves 6

3 lb/1.3 kg chicken

9½ cups beef stock

2 lb/900 g leeks

1 bouquet garni

salt and pepper

1 lb/450 g prunes, pitted and soaked overnight in enough cold water to cover

Method

❶ Place the chicken, breast-side down, in a large, heavy-bottom pan or ovenproof casserole. Pour in the stock and bring to a boil, skimming off any froth that rises to the surface.

❷ Tie half the leeks together in a bundle with kitchen string and thinly slice the remainder. Add the bundle of leeks to the pan with the bouquet garni and a pinch of salt. Reduce the heat, then partially cover and let simmer for 2 hours, or until the chicken is tender.

❸ Remove and discard the bundle of leeks and bouquet garni. Drain the prunes, add them to the pan, and let simmer for 20 minutes. Season to taste, then add the sliced leeks. Simmer for an additional 10 minutes. Slice the chicken, or cut into bite-size pieces, and serve at once.

Cook's tip

A bouquet garni usually consists of 3 fresh parsley sprigs, 2 fresh thyme sprigs, and a bay leaf, tied together in a bundle.

Bacon & Lentil Soup

Bacon and lentils have a real affinity—their flavors and textures complement one another. This popular family supper also includes a selection of tasty winter vegetables.

serves 4–6

1 lb/450 g thick, rindless smoked bacon slices, diced

1 onion, chopped

2 carrots, sliced

2 celery stalks, chopped

1 turnip, chopped

1 large potato, chopped

scant ½ cup Puy lentils

1 bouquet garni

4 cups water or chicken stock

salt and pepper

Method

❶ Heat a large, heavy-bottom pan or ovenproof casserole. Add the bacon and cook over medium heat, stirring, for 4–5 minutes, or until the fat runs. Add the chopped onion, carrots, celery, turnip, and potato and cook, stirring frequently, for 5 minutes.

❷ Add the lentils and bouquet garni and pour in the water. Bring to a boil, reduce the heat, and let simmer for 1 hour, or until the lentils are tender.

❸ Remove and discard the bouquet garni and season the soup to taste with pepper, and with salt, if necessary. Ladle into warmed soup bowls and serve at once.

Cook's tip

Do not add any salt until the lentils have finished cooking, or they will toughen, which will impair the texture of the soup.

Beef & Vegetable Soup

This colorful, spicy soup comes from Southeast Asia, where it would
be served with plain boiled rice, but it is substantial enough to make
a filling meal on its own.

serves 6

2 tbsp peanut or corn oil	½-inch/1-cm cube shrimp paste (optional)
1 large onion, finely chopped	4 cups chicken or beef stock
½ cup fresh lean ground beef	salt
1 garlic clove, finely chopped	4 oz/115 g cooked shelled shrimp
2 fresh red chiles, seeded	5 cups fresh spinach, coarse stems
and finely chopped	removed and leaves shredded
1 tbsp ground almonds	6 oz/175 g baby corn, sliced
1 carrot, grated	1 beefsteak tomato, chopped
1 tsp brown sugar	2 tbsp lime juice

Method

❶ Heat the oil in a large, heavy-bottom pan. Add the onion and cook over low heat, stirring occasionally, for 5 minutes, or until softened. Add the beef and garlic and cook, stirring, until the meat is browned.

❷ Add the chiles, ground almonds, grated carrot, and sugar. Add the shrimp paste (if using). Pour in the stock and season to taste with salt. Bring the mixture to a boil over low heat, then let simmer for 10 minutes.

❸ Stir in the shrimp, spinach, baby corn, tomato, and lime juice. Let the mixture simmer for an additional 2–3 minutes, or until heated through. Ladle into warmed bowls and serve at once.

Variation

Replace the shrimp with 2 oz/55 g of dried shrimp soaked in hot water for 10 minutes. Add the shrimp and soaking water with the stock in Step 2.

Beef Stroganoff

This traditional Slavic recipe makes a comforting meal on a chilly evening. Thin strips of delicately cooked beef and a mustard and cream sauce make this simple dish taste out of the ordinary.

serves 4

⅛ cup dried porcini

12 oz/350 g sirloin steak

2 tbsp olive oil

4 oz/115 g shallots, sliced

6 oz/175 g cremini mushrooms

salt and pepper

½ tsp Dijon mustard

5 tbsp heavy cream

fresh chives, to garnish

freshly cooked pasta, to serve

Method

❶ Place the dried porcini in a bowl and cover with hot water. Let soak for 20 minutes. Meanwhile, cut the beef against the grain into ¼-inch/5-mm thick slices, then into ½-inch/1-cm long strips, and set aside.

❷ Drain the porcini, reserving the soaking liquid, and chop. Strain the soaking liquid through a fine mesh strainer or coffee filter and set aside.

❸ Heat half the oil in a large skillet. Add the shallots and cook over low heat, stirring occasionally, for 5 minutes, or until softened. Add the porcini, reserved soaking water, and whole cremini mushrooms. Cook, stirring frequently, for 10 minutes, or until almost all of the liquid has evaporated, then transfer the mixture to a plate.

❹ Heat the remaining oil in the skillet, add the beef, and cook, stirring frequently, for 4 minutes, or until browned all over. You may need to do this in batches. Return the mushroom mixture to the skillet and season to taste.

❺ Place the mustard and cream in a small bowl and stir to mix, then fold into the mixture. Heat through gently, then serve with pasta, garnished with chives.

Beef in Beer with Herb Dumplings

Serve this traditional stew with its topping of satisfying dumplings to counteract even the coldest winter weather.

serves 6

2 tbsp corn oil

2 large onions, thinly sliced

8 carrots, sliced

4 tbsp all-purpose flour

salt and pepper

2 lb 12 oz/1.25 kg stewing steak, cut into cubes

scant 2 cups stout

2 tsp brown sugar

2 bay leaves

1 tbsp chopped fresh thyme

Herb dumplings

¾ cup self-rising flour

pinch of salt

½ cup shredded shortening

2 tbsp chopped fresh parsley, plus extra to garnish

about 4 tbsp water

Method

❶ Preheat the oven to 325°F/160°C. Heat the oil in an ovenproof casserole. Add the onions and carrots and cook over low heat, stirring occasionally, for 5 minutes, or until the onions are softened. Meanwhile, place the flour in a plastic bag and season. Add the steak to the bag, tie the top, and shake well to coat. Do this in batches, if necessary.

❷ Remove the vegetables from the casserole with a slotted spoon and set aside. Add the steak to the casserole, in batches, and cook, stirring frequently, until browned all over. Return the meat, onions, and carrots to the casserole and sprinkle in any remaining seasoned flour. Pour in the stout and add the sugar, bay leaves, and thyme. Bring to a boil, cover, and bake in the preheated oven for 1¾ hours.

❸ To make the Herb Dumplings, sift the flour and salt into a bowl. Stir in the shortening and parsley, then add enough water to make a dough. Shape into small balls. Add to the casserole and return to the oven for 30 minutes. Remove the bay leaves. Serve, sprinkled with parsley.

Stifado

This wonderful traditional Greek stew is cooked very slowly with the result
that the beef almost melts in the mouth and all the flavors mingle in a rich, thick,
delicious gravy.

serves 6

1 lb/450 g tomatoes, peeled

⅔ cup beef stock

2 tbsp olive oil

1 lb/450 g shallots, peeled

2 garlic cloves, finely chopped

1 lb 9 oz/700 g stewing steak,
cut into 1-inch/2.5-cm cubes

1 fresh rosemary sprig

1 bay leaf

2 tbsp red wine vinegar

salt and pepper

1 lb/450 g potatoes, quartered

Method

❶ Place the tomatoes in a blender or food processor, add the stock, and process to a purée. Alternatively, push them through a strainer into a bowl with the back of a wooden spoon and mix with the stock.

❷ Heat the oil in a large, heavy-bottom pan or ovenproof casserole. Add the shallots and garlic and cook over low heat, stirring occasionally, for 8 minutes, or until golden. Transfer to a plate with a slotted spoon. Add the steak to the pan and cook, stirring frequently, for 5–8 minutes, or until browned.

❸ Return the shallots and garlic to the pan, add the tomato mixture, herbs, and vinegar, and season to taste. Cover and let simmer gently for 1½ hours. Add the potatoes, cover, and let simmer for an additional 30 minutes. Remove and discard the rosemary and bay leaf. Serve.

Cook's tip

*Fresh, uncooked rosemary sprigs and bay leaves
would make an attractive garnish for this dish,
but remember to remove them before eating.*

Irish Stew

Nothing could be simpler, tastier, or more economical than this traditional,
warming stew. Serve with fresh soda bread for an authentic touch—
and to mop up the delicious juices.

serves 4

4 tbsp all-purpose flour

salt and pepper

3 lb/1.3 kg middle neck of lamb,

cut into chop-size pieces, and

trimmed of excess fat

3 large onions, chopped

3 carrots, sliced

1 lb/450 g potatoes, quartered

½ tsp dried thyme

3½ cups beef stock

2 tbsp chopped fresh parsley,

to garnish

Method

❶ Preheat the oven to 325°F/160°C.
Spread the flour on a plate and season.
Roll the pieces of lamb in the flour to
coat, shaking off any excess, and arrange
in the bottom of a casserole.

❷ Layer the onions, carrots, and potatoes
on top of the lamb.

❸ Sprinkle in the thyme and pour in
the stock, then cover and cook in the
preheated oven for 2½ hours. Garnish
with the chopped fresh parsley and serve
straight from the casserole.

Cook's tip

*This stew is even more substantial and flavorsome
if it is served with Herb Dumplings (see page 18).
Add them to the casserole 30 minutes before the
end of the cooking time.*

Moroccan Lamb

Slow-cooking lamb with dried fruit and spices is traditional in North Africa.
Stews flavored with dried fruits, including apricots and prunes, have now
become familiar elsewhere.

serves 4

1 lb 2 oz/500 g boneless leg of lamb

1 tbsp corn oil

12 oz/350 g shallots, peeled but left whole

scant 2 cups chicken stock

1 tbsp honey

1 tsp ground cinnamon

½ tsp ground ginger

½ tsp saffron threads, lightly crushed

¼ tsp freshly grated nutmeg

salt and pepper

grated rind and juice of 1 small orange,
plus extra rind to garnish

12 no-soak prunes

Method

❶ Cut the lamb into large cubes. Heat the oil in an ovenproof casserole, then add the lamb and cook over medium heat, stirring, for 3–5 minutes, or until browned. Transfer to a plate. Add the shallots to the casserole and cook over low heat, stirring occasionally, for 10 minutes, or until golden. Transfer them to a separate plate with a slotted spoon.

❷ Pour away any excess fat from the casserole, then add the stock and bring to a boil, stirring constantly and scraping up any sediment from the bottom. Return the lamb to the casserole and stir in the honey, cinnamon, ginger, saffron, and nutmeg. Season to taste, then cover and let simmer for 30 minutes.

❸ Return the shallots to the casserole and add the orange rind and juice. Cover and let simmer for an additional 30 minutes. Add the prunes and adjust the seasoning, if necessary. Let simmer, uncovered, for an additional 15 minutes. Garnish with orange rind and serve at once.

Cook's tip

"No-soak" fruit requires no advance preparation.
You can also find packages of moist,
"ready-to-eat" fruit in most supermarkets.

French Country Casserole

A crispy potato topping covers a dish of succulent, tender lamb, flavored with mint, leeks, and apricots in this traditional rustic casserole—which tastes as good as it looks.

serves 6

2 tbsp corn oil

4 lb 8 oz/2 kg boneless leg of lamb, cut into 1-inch/2.5-cm cubes

6 leeks, sliced

1 tbsp all-purpose flour

²/₃ cup blush wine

1¼ cups chicken stock

1 tbsp tomato paste

1 tbsp sugar

2 tbsp chopped fresh mint

²/₃ cup dried apricots, chopped

salt and pepper

2 lb 4 oz/1 kg potatoes, sliced

3 tbsp melted unsalted butter

fresh mint sprigs, to garnish

Method

❶ Preheat the oven to 350°F/180°C. Heat the oil in a large, ovenproof casserole. Add the lamb in batches and cook over medium heat, stirring, for 5–8 minutes, or until browned. Transfer to a plate.

❷ Add the sliced leeks to the casserole and cook, stirring occasionally, for 5 minutes, or until softened. Sprinkle in the flour and cook, stirring, for 1 minute. Pour in the wine and stock and bring to a boil, stirring. Stir in the tomato paste, sugar, chopped mint, and apricots and season to taste.

❸ Return the lamb to the casserole and stir. Arrange the potato slices on top and brush with the melted butter. Cover and bake in the preheated oven for 1½ hours.

❹ Increase the oven temperature to 400°F/200°C, then uncover the casserole and bake for an additional 30 minutes, or until the potato topping is golden brown. Serve at once, garnished with fresh mint sprigs.

Paprika Pork

This is a good dish for entertaining, as it can be prepared in advance and stored in the refrigerator for up to two days. To serve, reheat gently, then stir in the sour cream.

serves 4

1 lb 8 oz/675 g pork fillet

2 tbsp corn oil

2 tbsp butter

1 onion, chopped

1 tbsp paprika

2 tbsp all-purpose flour

1 1/4 cups chicken stock

4 tbsp dry sherry

4 oz/115 g mushrooms, sliced

salt and pepper

2/3 cup sour cream

Method

❶ Cut the pork into 1½-inch/4-cm cubes. Heat the oil and butter in a large pan. Add the pork and cook over medium heat, stirring, for 5 minutes, or until browned. Transfer the pork to a plate with a slotted spoon.

❷ Add the chopped onion to the pan and cook, stirring occasionally, for 5 minutes, or until softened. Stir in the paprika and flour and cook, stirring constantly, for 2 minutes. Gradually stir in the stock and bring to a boil, stirring constantly.

❸ Return the pork to the pan, add the sherry and sliced mushrooms, and season to taste. Cover and let simmer gently for 20 minutes, or until the pork is tender. Stir in the sour cream and serve.

Cook's tip

There are two kinds of paprika—sweet and hot—but both are much milder than cayenne pepper. Sweet paprika is the best choice for this recipe.

Pot-Roast Pork

Beef and chicken are the most popular choices for pot roasting, but a loin of pork works superbly well, too. This is a rich and flavorsome dish that is ideal for entertaining.

serves 4

1 tbsp corn oil

2 oz/55 g butter

2 lb 4 oz/1 kg boned and rolled pork loin

4 shallots, chopped

6 juniper berries

2 fresh thyme sprigs, plus extra to garnish

^{2}/$_3$ cup hard cider

^{2}/$_3$ cup chicken stock or water

salt and pepper

8 celery stalks, chopped

2 tbsp all-purpose flour

^{2}/$_3$ cup heavy cream

freshly cooked peas, to serve

Method

❶ Heat the oil with half the butter in a heavy-bottom pan or ovenproof casserole. Add the pork and cook over medium heat, turning frequently, for 5–10 minutes, or until browned. Transfer to a plate.

❷ Add the shallots to the pan and cook, stirring frequently, for 5 minutes, or until softened. Add the juniper berries and thyme sprigs and return the pork to the pan, with any juices that have collected on the plate. Pour in the cider and stock, season to taste, then cover and let simmer for 30 minutes. Turn the pork over and add the celery. Cover the pan and cook for an additional 40 minutes.

❸ Meanwhile, make a beurre manié by mashing the remaining butter with the flour in a small bowl. Transfer the pork and celery to a plate with a slotted spoon and keep warm. Remove and discard the juniper berries and thyme.

❹ Whisk the beurre manié, a little at a time, into the simmering cooking liquid. Cook, stirring constantly, for 2 minutes, then stir in the cream and bring to a boil. Slice the pork and spoon a little of the sauce over it. Garnish with thyme sprigs and serve at once with the celery and freshly cooked peas. Hand round the remaining sauce separately.

Brunswick Stew

This traditional chicken stew is a hearty dish, which is suffused with warm, spicy undertones. Serve it with salad and whole-wheat rolls to make a filling, warming winter supper.

serves 6

4 lb/1.8 kg chicken pieces

salt

2 tbsp paprika

2 tbsp olive oil

2 tbsp butter

1 lb/450 g onions, chopped

2 yellow bell peppers, seeded and chopped

14 oz/400 g canned chopped tomatoes

1 cup dry white wine

2 cups chicken stock

1 tbsp Worcestershire sauce

½ tsp Tabasco sauce

1 tbsp finely chopped fresh parsley

11½ oz/325 g canned corn kernels, drained

15 oz/425 g canned lima beans, drained and rinsed

2 tbsp all-purpose flour

4 tbsp water

fresh parsley sprigs, to garnish

Method

❶ Season the chicken pieces with salt and dust with paprika.

❷ Heat the oil and butter in an ovenproof casserole or large pan. Add the chicken pieces and cook over medium heat, turning, for 10–15 minutes, or until golden. Transfer the chicken to a plate using a slotted spoon.

❸ Add the onion and bell peppers to the casserole. Cook over low heat, stirring occasionally, for 5 minutes, or until softened. Add the tomatoes, wine, stock, Worcestershire sauce, Tabasco sauce, and parsley and bring to a boil, stirring. Return the chicken to the casserole, then cover and let simmer, stirring occasionally, for 30 minutes.

❹ Add the corn and beans to the casserole, partially cover, and let simmer for an additional 30 minutes. Place the flour and water in a small bowl and mix to make a paste. Stir a ladleful of the cooking liquid into the paste, then stir it into the stew. Cook, stirring frequently, for 5 minutes. Serve, garnished with parsley.

Jambalaya

This Cajun dish is borrowed from Spain, where it originated. Its lively mixture of chicken and shrimp makes it a good dish to serve at a brunch party, instead of the more traditional kedgeree.

serves 6

2 tbsp shortening

3 lb 5 oz/1.5 kg chicken pieces

2 tbsp all-purpose flour

8 oz/225 g rindless smoked ham, diced

1 onion, chopped

1 orange bell pepper, seeded and sliced

12 oz/350 g tomatoes, peeled and chopped

1 garlic clove, finely chopped

1 tsp chopped fresh thyme

12 jumbo shrimp, shelled

generous 1 cup long-grain rice

2 cups chicken stock or water

dash of Tabasco sauce

salt and pepper

3 scallions, finely chopped

2 tbsp chopped fresh flatleaf parsley

fresh flatleaf parsley sprigs, to garnish

Method

❶ Melt the shortening in a large, ovenproof casserole. Add the chicken and cook over medium heat, turning occasionally, for 8–10 minutes, or until golden brown all over. Transfer the chicken to a plate using a slotted spoon.

❷ Add the flour and cook over very low heat, stirring, for 15 minutes, or until golden brown. Do not let it burn. Return the chicken pieces to the casserole with the ham, onion, orange bell pepper, tomatoes, garlic, and thyme. Cook, stirring frequently, for 10 minutes.

❸ Stir in the shrimp, rice, and stock and season to taste with Tabasco, salt, and pepper. Bring the mixture to a boil, then reduce the heat and cook for 15–20 minutes, or until all of the liquid has been absorbed and the rice is tender. Stir in the scallions and chopped parsley, garnish with parsley sprigs, and serve at once.

Variation

If you don't want to use shortening in this recipe, substitute 2 tablespoons of corn oil at the beginning of Step 1.

Chicken Pasanda

This Balti dish is traditionally cooked and served in a karahi—a pan similar in shape to a wok. If you have neither a karahi nor a wok, use a large, heavy-bottom skillet instead.

serves 4

4 cardamom pods

6 black peppercorns

½ cinnamon stick

½ tsp cumin seeds

2 tsp garam masala

1 tsp chili powder

1 tsp grated fresh gingerroot

1 garlic clove, very finely chopped

4 tbsp thick plain yogurt

pinch of salt

1 lb 8 oz/675 g skinless, boneless chicken, diced

5 tbsp peanut oil

2 onions, finely chopped

3 fresh green chiles, seeded and chopped

2 tbsp chopped fresh cilantro

½ cup light cream

fresh cilantro sprigs, to garnish

Method

❶ Place the cardamom pods in a nonmetallic dish with the peppercorns, cinnamon, cumin, garam masala, chili powder, ginger, garlic, yogurt, and salt. Add the diced chicken and stir well to coat. Cover and let marinate in the refrigerator for 2–3 hours.

❷ Heat the oil in a preheated wok or karahi. Add the onions and cook over low heat, stirring occasionally, for 5 minutes, or until softened, then add the chicken pieces and marinade and cook over medium heat, stirring, for 15 minutes, or until the chicken is cooked through.

❸ Stir in the fresh chiles and cilantro and pour in the cream. Heat through gently, but do not let it boil. Garnish with fresh cilantro and serve at once.

Coq au Vin

Traditional recipes often yield wonderfully tasty results, and this dish is no exception. Serve this perennial favorite with warm French bread or garlic bread to mop up the delicious wine-flavored juices.

serves 4

2 oz/55 g butter

2 tbsp olive oil

4 lb/1.8 kg chicken pieces

4 oz/115 g rindless smoked bacon,
cut into strips

4 oz/115 g pearl onions

4 oz/115 g cremini mushrooms, halved

2 garlic cloves, finely chopped

2 tbsp brandy

1 cup red wine

1¼ cups chicken stock

1 bouquet garni

salt and pepper

2 tbsp all-purpose flour

bay leaves, to garnish

Method

❶ Melt half the butter with the olive oil in a large, ovenproof casserole. Add the chicken and cook over medium heat, stirring, for 8–10 minutes, or until golden brown all over. Add the bacon, onions, mushrooms, and garlic.

❷ Pour in the brandy and set it alight with a match or taper. When the flames have died down, add the wine, stock, and bouquet garni and season to taste. Bring to a boil, reduce the heat, and let simmer gently for 1 hour, or until the chicken pieces are cooked through and tender. Meanwhile, make a beurre manié by mashing the remaining butter with the flour in a small bowl.

❸ Remove and discard the bouquet garni. Transfer the chicken to a large plate and keep warm. Stir the beurre manié into the casserole, a little at a time. Bring to a boil, return the chicken to the casserole, and serve at once, garnished with bay leaves.

Cook's tip

If you like, cook the chicken in the oven instead of on the stove. Transfer it to a preheated oven, 325°F/160°C, once the mixture has come to a boil in Step 2. Cook for 1 hour, then follow Step 3.

Mexican Turkey

Using chocolate in savory dishes is a Mexican tradition and, while it may sound strange, it gives the meat a very rich flavor. Mexican chocolate often has cinnamon incorporated into it, but you can use ordinary semisweet chocolate and ground cinnamon for this dish.

serves 4

3/8 cup all-purpose flour

salt and pepper

4 turkey breast fillets

3 tbsp corn oil

1 onion, thinly sliced

1 red bell pepper, seeded and sliced

1¼ cups chicken stock

1 heaping tbsp raisins

4 tomatoes, peeled, seeded and chopped

1 tsp chili powder

½ tsp ground cinnamon

pinch of ground cumin

1 oz/25 g semisweet chocolate, finely chopped or grated

chopped fresh cilantro, to garnish

Method

❶ Preheat the oven to 325°F/160°C. Spread the flour on a plate and season. Coat the turkey fillets in the seasoned flour, shaking off any excess.

❷ Heat the oil in an ovenproof casserole. Add the turkey fillets and cook over medium heat, turning occasionally, for 5–10 minutes, or until golden. Transfer to a plate using a slotted spoon.

❸ Add the onion and red bell pepper to the casserole. Cook over low heat, stirring occasionally, for 5 minutes, or until softened. Sprinkle in any remaining seasoned flour and cook, stirring constantly, for 1 minute. Gradually stir in the stock, then add the raisins, chopped tomatoes, chili powder, cinnamon, cumin, and chocolate. Season to taste. Bring to a boil, stirring constantly.

❹ Return the turkey to the casserole, cover, and cook in the preheated oven for 50 minutes. Serve at once, garnished with cilantro.

Cook's tip

For true flavor, choose the best quality semisweet chocolate you can find for this dish. It should contain a minimum of 70 percent cocoa solids.

Italian Turkey Steaks

This lively summer dish is simplicity itself, but tastes really wonderful and makes a surprisingly substantial main course.

serves 4

1 tbsp olive oil

4 turkey scallops or steaks

2 red bell peppers, seeded and sliced

1 red onion, sliced

2 garlic cloves, finely chopped

1¼ cups strained tomatoes

⅔ cup medium white wine

1 tbsp chopped fresh marjoram

salt and pepper

14 oz/400 g canned cannellini beans, drained and rinsed

3 tbsp fresh white bread crumbs

fresh basil sprigs, to garnish

Method

❶ Heat the oil in an ovenproof casserole or heavy-bottom skillet. Add the turkey scallops and cook over medium heat for 5–10 minutes, turning occasionally, until golden. Transfer to a plate.

❷ Add the bell peppers and onion to the skillet and cook over low heat, stirring occasionally, for 5 minutes, or until softened. Add the garlic and cook for an additional 2 minutes.

❸ Return the turkey to the skillet and add the strained tomatoes, wine, and marjoram. Season to taste with salt and pepper. Bring to a boil, then reduce the heat, cover, and let simmer, stirring occasionally, for 25–30 minutes, or until the turkey is cooked through and tender.

❹ Preheat the broiler to medium. Stir in the cannellini beans and simmer for an additional 5 minutes. Sprinkle the bread crumbs over the top and place under the hot broiler for 2–3 minutes, until golden. Serve, garnished with fresh basil sprigs.

Variation

Soak ⅛ cup of dried porcini mushrooms in boiling water to cover for 20 minutes. Drain and slice, then add with the onion and bell peppers in Step 2.

Seafood Risotto

The secret of a successful risotto is to use round grain Italian rice, such as Arborio, and to add a ladleful of stock at a time, making sure that it is fully absorbed before more is added.

serves 4

12 oz/350 g skinless cod fillet, cut into cubes

2 tbsp unsalted butter

1 onion, chopped

2 red bell peppers, seeded and chopped

4 tomatoes, peeled, seeded, and chopped

8 ready-prepared scallops

2 tbsp olive oil

generous 1 cup risotto rice

2 cups hot fish stock

salt

8 oz/225 g cooked shelled shrimp

1 tbsp chopped flatleaf parsley

2 tbsp freshly grated Parmesan cheese

fresh parsley sprigs, to garnish

Method

❶ Melt half the butter in a large pan. Add the chopped onion, red bell peppers, and tomatoes and cook over low heat, stirring occasionally, for 5 minutes, or until softened. Add the cubed fish and the scallops, and cook for an additional 3 minutes. Transfer the fish mixture to a plate using a slotted spoon, then cover and set aside.

❷ Add the oil and the remaining butter to the pan and heat gently. Add the rice and stir to coat with the butter and oil. Stir in a ladleful of stock and season to taste with salt. Cook, stirring, until the stock has been absorbed. Continue cooking and adding stock, a ladleful at a time, for 20 minutes, or until the rice is tender and all of the liquid has been absorbed.

❸ Gently stir in the reserved fish mixture with the shrimp and heat through for 2 minutes. Transfer the risotto to a warmed serving dish, sprinkle with the parsley and Parmesan cheese, and serve at once, garnished with parsley sprigs.

Cook's tip

Risotto rice will absorb stock more readily if the stock is kept at simmering point in another pan while it is being added in Step 2.

Thai Shrimp Curry

Thai cooking is renowned for its subtle blending of aromatic spices,
and this mouthwatering curry is no exception.

serves 4

1 lb/450 g raw jumbo shrimp

2 tbsp peanut oil

2 tbsp Thai green curry paste

4 kaffir lime leaves, shredded

1 lemongrass stalk, chopped

1 cup coconut milk

2 tbsp Thai fish sauce

½ cucumber, seeded and cut into sticks

12 fresh basil leaves, plus extra to garnish

2 fresh green chiles, sliced

Method

❶ Shell and devein the shrimp. Heat the peanut oil in a preheated wok or heavy-bottom skillet. Add the curry paste and cook over medium heat for 1 minute, or until it is bubbling and releases its aroma.

❷ Add the shrimp, lime leaves, and lemongrass and stir-fry for 2 minutes, or until the shrimp have turned pink.

❸ Stir in the coconut milk and bring to a boil, then reduce the heat and let simmer, stirring occasionally, for 5 minutes. Stir in the fish sauce, cucumber, and basil. Transfer to a warmed serving dish. Sprinkle over the chile slices, garnish with fresh basil leaves, and serve.

Cook's tip

Three types of basil are used in Thailand: hairy (bai mangluk), sweet *(bai horapa), and Thai or holy basil (bai grapao). They are all more strongly flavored than Western basil.*

Paella del Mar

Paella is actually the name of the pan in which this famous Spanish dish is cooked—a large, heavy-bottom skillet or casserole is a good substitute.

serves 6

1 lb/450 g live mussels

6 squid

½ cup olive oil

1 Spanish onion, chopped

2 garlic cloves, finely chopped

1 red bell pepper, seeded and cut into strips

1 green bell pepper, seeded and cut into strips

scant 2 cups risotto rice

2 tomatoes, peeled and chopped

1 tbsp tomato paste

6 oz/175 g angler fish fillet, cut into chunks

6 oz/175 g red snapper fillet, cut into chunks

6 oz/175 g cod fillet, cut into chunks

scant 2½ cups fish stock

4 oz/115 g green beans, halved

4 oz/115 g fresh or frozen peas

6 canned artichoke hearts, drained

¼ tsp saffron threads

salt and pepper

12 raw jumbo shrimp

Method

❶ Clean the mussels by scrubbing the shells and pulling off any beards. Discard any with broken shells or any that refuse to close when tapped with a knife. Rinse the mussels under cold running water.

❷ To prepare each squid, pull the pouch and tentacles apart, then remove the innards from the pouch. Slice the tentacles away from the head and discard the head. Rinse the pouch and tentacles under cold running water.

❸ Heat the oil in a paella pan. Add the onion, garlic, and bell peppers and cook over medium heat, stirring, for 5 minutes, or until softened. Add the squid and cook for 2 minutes. Add the rice and cook until transparent and coated with oil.

❹ Add the tomatoes, tomato paste, and fish and cook for 3 minutes, then add the stock. Stir in the beans, peas, artichoke hearts, and saffron and season to taste.

❺ Arrange the mussels round the edge of the pan, then top the mixture with the shrimp. Bring to a boil, reduce the heat and let simmer, shaking the pan from time to time, for 15–20 minutes, until the rice is tender. Discard any mussels that remain closed. Serve straight from the pan.

Moules Marinières

Served with plenty of fresh crusty French bread, this is a shellfish-lover's feast. The only extra treat you need to make this into a perfect meal is a glass of chilled white wine.

serves 4

4 lb 8 oz/2 kg live mussels

1¼ cups dry white wine

6 shallots, finely chopped

1 bouquet garni

pepper

crusty bread, to serve

Method

❶ Clean the mussels by scrubbing the shells and pulling off any beards. Discard any with broken shells or any that refuse to close when tapped with a knife. Rinse the mussels under cold running water.

❷ Pour the wine into a large, heavy-bottom pan, add the shallots and bouquet garni, and season to taste with pepper. Bring to a boil over medium heat. Add the mussels, cover tightly, and cook, shaking the pan occasionally, for 5 minutes. Remove and discard the bouquet garni and any mussels that remain closed.

❸ Divide the mussels between 4 soup bowls with a slotted spoon. Tilt the casserole to let any sand settle, then spoon the cooking liquid over the mussels and serve at once with bread.

Cook's tip

Never eat mussels that you have collected from the beach yourself, as they may have been polluted and could cause serious illness.

Boston Fish Pie

Boston has been described as "the home of the bean and the cod." This may
not sound glamorous, but this unusual fish pie does demonstrate that
it is a tasty and filling combination.

serves 6

2 tbsp butter, plus extra for greasing

2 onions, chopped

2 lb 4 oz/1 kg cod fillet, skinned
and cut into strips

4 rindless lean bacon slices,
cut into strips

2 tbsp chopped fresh parsley

salt and pepper

14 oz/400 g canned Great Northern beans,
drained and rinsed

2½ cups milk

1 lb 2 oz/500 g potatoes,
very thinly sliced

fresh parsley sprigs, to garnish

Method

❶ Preheat the oven to 350°F/180°C.
Lightly grease an ovenproof casserole with
a little butter. Arrange the chopped onions
on the bottom and then cover with the
strips of fish and bacon. Sprinkle with the
chopped parsley and season to taste.

❷ Add the Great Northern beans, then
pour in the milk. Arrange the potato slices,
overlapping them slightly, to cover the
entire surface of the pie.

❸ Dot the potato slices with the butter.
Bake the pie in the preheated oven for
40 minutes, or until the potatoes are crisp
and golden. Garnish with parsley sprigs
and serve at once.

Cook's tip

*If you like, before baking in the oven, cover the
casserole with aluminum foil, then remove the foil
for the last 10 minutes of cooking time to crisp up
the potatoes.*

Vegetarian

Corn, Potato & Cheese Soup

This easy-to-make, satisfying soup is put together mainly with pantry ingredients. It is the perfect choice for a Sunday brunch, as it takes very little effort or concentration.

serves 4

2 tbsp butter

2 shallots, finely chopped

8 oz/225 g potatoes, diced

4 tbsp all-purpose flour

2 tbsp dry white wine

1¼ cups milk

11½ oz/325 g canned corn kernels, drained

3 oz/85 g Gruyère, Emmental, or Cheddar cheese, grated

8–10 fresh sage leaves, chopped

scant 2 cups heavy cream

fresh sage sprigs, to garnish

Croutons

2–3 slices of day-old white bread

2 tbsp olive oil

Method

❶ To make the croutons, cut the crusts off the slices of bread, then cut the remaining bread into ¼-inch/5-mm squares. Heat the olive oil in a heavy-bottom skillet and add the bread cubes. Cook, tossing and stirring constantly, until evenly colored. Drain the croutons thoroughly on paper towels and set aside.

❷ Melt the butter in a large, heavy-bottom pan. Add the shallots and cook over low heat, stirring occasionally, for 5 minutes, or until softened. Add the potatoes and cook, stirring, for 2 minutes.

❸ Sprinkle in the flour and cook, stirring, for 1 minute. Remove the pan from the heat and stir in the white wine, then gradually stir in the milk. Return the pan to the heat and bring to a boil, stirring constantly, then reduce the heat and let simmer.

❹ Stir in the corn kernels, grated cheese, chopped sage, and cream and heat through gently until the cheese has just melted. Ladle the soup into warmed bowls, sprinkle over the croutons, garnish with fresh sage sprigs, and serve at once.

Cauliflower Bake

The bright red of the tomatoes is a great contrast to the colors of the cauliflower and herbs in this dish, making it appealing to both the eye and the palate. It is easy to prepare and satisfying to eat.

serves 4

1 lb 2 oz/500 g cauliflower, broken into florets

1 lb 5 oz/600 g potatoes, cut into cubes

3½ oz/100 g cherry tomatoes

chopped fresh flatleaf parsley, to garnish

Sauce

2 tbsp butter or margarine

1 leek, sliced

1 garlic clove, crushed

3 tbsp all-purpose flour

1¼ cups milk

3 oz/85 g mixed cheese, such as Cheddar, Parmesan, or Gruyère, grated

½ tsp paprika

2 tbsp chopped fresh flatleaf parsley

salt and pepper

Method

❶ Preheat the oven to 350°F/180°C. Cook the cauliflower florets in a pan of boiling water for 10 minutes. Meanwhile, cook the potato cubes in another pan of boiling water for 10 minutes. Drain both vegetables and set aside.

❷ To make the sauce, melt the butter in a large, heavy-bottom pan, add the leek and garlic, and cook over low heat for 1 minute. Stir in the flour and cook, stirring constantly, for 1 minute. Remove the pan from the heat, then gradually stir in the milk, ½ cup of the grated cheese, the paprika, and the parsley. Return the

pan to the heat and bring to a boil, stirring constantly. Season to taste with salt and pepper.

❸ Transfer the cauliflower to a deep, ovenproof dish with the cherry tomatoes, and top with the potatoes. Pour the sauce over the potatoes and sprinkle over the remaining grated cheese.

❹ Cook in the preheated oven for 20 minutes, or until the vegetables are cooked through and the cheese is golden brown and bubbling. Garnish with chopped parsley and serve at once.

Bell Pepper &
Mushroom Hash

This quick and easy-to-prepare one-pan dish is ideal for an evening snack. Packed with color and flavor, it is an extremely versatile recipe—you can add whichever vegetables you have to hand.

serves 4

1 lb 8 oz/675 g potatoes, cut into cubes

1 tbsp olive oil

2 garlic cloves, crushed

1 green bell pepper, seeded and cut into cubes

1 yellow bell pepper, seeded and cut into cubes

3 tomatoes, diced

2¾ oz/75 g white mushrooms, halved

1 tbsp Worcestershire sauce

2 tbsp chopped fresh basil

salt and pepper

fresh basil sprigs, to garnish

warm crusty bread, to serve

Method

❶ Cook the potato cubes in a pan of lightly salted boiling water for 7–8 minutes. Drain well and set aside.

❷ Heat the olive oil in a large, heavy-bottom skillet. Add the potato cubes and cook over medium heat, stirring, for 8–10 minutes, or until browned.

❸ Add the crushed garlic and bell pepper cubes and cook, stirring frequently, for 2–3 minutes. Add the tomatoes and mushrooms and cook, stirring frequently, for 5–6 minutes.

❹ Stir in the Worcestershire sauce and basil and season to taste with salt and pepper. Transfer to a warmed serving dish, garnish with basil leaves, and serve with warm crusty bread.

Cook's tip

Most brands of Worcestershire sauce contain anchovies, so if you are a vegetarian, check the label to make sure you choose a vegetarian variety.

Winter Cobbler

Seasonal vegetables are casseroled with lentils, then topped with cheese biscuits.

serves 4

1 tbsp olive oil	2 tsp Tabasco sauce
1 garlic clove, crushed	2 tsp chopped fresh oregano
8 small onions, halved	fresh oregano sprigs, to garnish
2 celery stalks, sliced	
8 oz/225 g rutabaga, chopped	**Topping**
½ small cauliflower, broken into florets	1½ cups self-rising flour
2 carrots, sliced	pinch of salt
8 oz/225 g mushrooms, sliced	4 tbsp butter
14 oz/400 g canned chopped tomatoes	4 oz/115 g sharp Cheddar cheese, grated
2 oz/55 g red split lentils, rinsed	2 tsp chopped fresh oregano
2 tbsp cornstarch	1 egg, lightly beaten
3–4 tbsp water	⅔ cup milk
1¼ cups vegetable stock	

Method

❶ Preheat the oven to 350°F/180°C. Heat the olive oil in a large skillet and cook the crushed garlic and the halved onions over low heat for 5 minutes. Add the celery, rutabaga, cauliflower florets, and carrots to the skillet and cook for 2–3 minutes.

❷ Add the mushrooms, tomatoes, and lentils to the skillet. Place the cornstarch and water in a bowl and mix to make a smooth paste. Stir into the skillet with the vegetable stock, Tabasco, and oregano. Transfer to an ovenproof dish, cover, and bake in the preheated oven for 20 minutes.

❸ To make the topping, sift the flour and salt into a bowl. Rub in the butter, then stir in most of the cheese and the chopped oregano. Beat the egg with the milk in a small bowl and add enough to the dry ingredients to make a soft dough. Knead, then roll out to ½-inch/1-cm thick and cut into 2-inch/5-cm circles.

❹ Remove the dish from the oven and increase the temperature to 400°F/200°C. Arrange the dough round the edge, brush with the remaining egg mixture, and sprinkle with the reserved cheese. Cook for 10–12 minutes. Garnish with oregano sprigs and serve.

Potato-Topped Vegetables

This dish is packed full of crunchy vegetables and coated in a white wine sauce.

serves 4

1 carrot, diced

6 oz/175 g cauliflower florets

6 oz/175 g broccoli florets

1 fennel bulb, sliced

3 oz/85 g green beans, halved

2 tbsp butter

2 tbsp all-purpose flour

²⁄₃ cup vegetable stock

²⁄₃ cup dry white wine

²⁄₃ cup milk

6 oz/175 g cremini mushrooms, quartered

2 tbsp chopped fresh sage

Topping

2 lb/900 g mealy potatoes, diced

2 tbsp butter

4 tbsp plain yogurt

⅝ cup freshly grated

Parmesan cheese

1 tsp fennel seeds

salt and pepper

Method

❶ Preheat the oven to 375°F/190°C. Cook the carrot, cauliflower, broccoli, fennel, and beans in a pan of boiling water for 10 minutes, or until just tender. Drain the vegetables and set aside.

❷ Melt the butter in a pan. Stir in the flour and cook over low heat for 1 minute. Remove from the heat and stir in the stock, wine, and milk. Return to the heat and bring to a boil, stirring, until thickened. Stir in the reserved vegetables, mushrooms, and chopped sage.

❸ To make the topping, cook the diced potatoes in a pan of boiling salted water for 10–15 minutes. Drain and mash with the butter, yogurt, and half the Parmesan cheese. Stir in the fennel seeds and season to taste.

❹ Spoon the vegetable mixture into a 4-cup pie dish. Spoon the potato mixture over the top, sprinkle over the remaining cheese, and cook in the preheated oven for 30–35 minutes, or until golden. Serve at once.

Risotto Primavera

As evenings get longer, the days grow warmer, and the first spring vegetables ripen, this is the ideal choice for a midweek supper.

serves 4

4 oz/115 g asparagus spears, cut into short lengths

2 young carrots, thinly sliced

2 tbsp unsalted butter

2 tbsp olive oil

1 white onion, chopped

2 garlic cloves, finely chopped

generous 1 cup risotto rice

3 tbsp dry white wine

4 cups hot vegetable stock

2 oz/55 g white mushrooms, halved

salt and pepper

½ cup freshly grated Parmesan cheese, to serve

Method

❶ Blanch the asparagus and carrots in a large pan of boiling water and drain well.

❷ Melt the butter with the oil in a large, heavy-bottom pan. Add the onion and garlic and cook over low heat, stirring occasionally, for 5 minutes, or until softened. Add the rice and stir well to coat the grains with the butter and oil. Add the white wine and cook until the liquid has been fully absorbed.

❸ Add a ladleful of stock to the rice and cook, stirring, until the liquid has been absorbed. Continue cooking and adding the stock, a ladleful at a time, for 20 minutes, or until the rice is tender and all of the liquid has been absorbed.

❹ Gently stir in the asparagus, carrots, and mushrooms, season to taste, and cook for an additional 2 minutes, or until heated through. Serve at once, handing round the grated Parmesan cheese separately.

Cook's tip

White onions, which are very popular in Italy, are sweeter and milder than brown ones. Alternatively, you could use a red onion for this dish.

Vegetable Chili

This is a hearty and flavorsome dish that works well served on its own, and is delicious spooned over cooked rice or baked potatoes to make a more substantial meal.

serves 4

1 eggplant, cut into 1-inch/2.5-cm slices	½ tsp ground cumin
1 tbsp olive oil, plus extra for brushing	½ tsp dried oregano
1 large red or yellow onion, finely chopped	salt and pepper
2 red or yellow bell peppers, seeded and finely chopped	2 small zucchini, quartered lengthwise and sliced
3–4 garlic cloves, finely chopped or crushed	14 oz/400 g canned kidney beans, drained and rinsed
1 lb 12 oz/800 g canned chopped tomatoes	2 cups water
1 tbsp mild chili powder	1 tbsp tomato paste
	6 scallions, finely chopped
	4 oz/115 g Cheddar cheese, grated

Method

❶ Brush the eggplant slices on one side with oil. Heat half the oil in a skillet. Add the slices, oiled-side up, and cook over medium heat for 5–6 minutes, or until browned on one side. Turn the slices over and cook until browned. Transfer to a plate and cut into bite-size pieces.

❷ Heat the remaining oil in a large pan over medium heat. Add the chopped onion and bell peppers to the pan and cook, stirring occasionally, for 3–4 minutes, or until the onion is softened but not browned. Add the garlic and cook for an additional 2–3 minutes, or until the onion starts to color.

❸ Add the tomatoes, chili powder, cumin, and oregano to the pan, then season to taste. Bring just to a boil, reduce the heat, cover, and let simmer gently for 15 minutes.

❹ Add the zucchini, eggplant pieces, and kidney beans. Stir in the water and tomato paste. Return to a boil, then cover the pan and let simmer for an additional 45 minutes, or until the vegetables are tender. Taste and adjust the seasoning, if necessary.

❺ Ladle into warmed bowls and top with scallions and cheese.

Sweet & Sour Vegetables

This is a dish of Persian origin—not Chinese, as it sounds. Plump, diced eggplants are cooked and mixed with tomatoes, mint, sugar, and vinegar to give a unique combination of flavors.

serves 4

2 large eggplants

salt and pepper

6 tbsp olive oil

4 garlic cloves, crushed

1 onion, cut into eighths

4 large tomatoes, seeded and chopped

3 tbsp chopped fresh mint

⅔ cup vegetable stock

4 tsp brown sugar

2 tbsp red wine vinegar

1 tsp red pepper flakes

fresh mint sprigs, to garnish

Method

❶ Cut the eggplants into cubes. Put them in a strainer, sprinkle with plenty of salt, and let stand for 30 minutes to remove all the bitter juices. Rinse thoroughly under cold running water and pat dry with paper towels.

❷ Heat the oil in a large, heavy-bottom skillet. Add the eggplant and cook over medium heat, stirring, for 1–2 minutes, or until starting to color. Stir in the garlic and onion wedges and cook, stirring constantly, for an additional 2–3 minutes.

❸ Stir in the tomatoes, mint, and stock. Reduce the heat, cover, and let simmer for 15–20 minutes, or until the eggplant and onion are tender.

❹ Add the sugar, vinegar, and the pepper flakes, then season to taste and cook for an additional 2–3 minutes, stirring.

❺ Transfer to a warmed serving dish, garnish with fresh mint sprigs, and serve at once.

Cook's tip

Choose firm, glossy eggplants for this dish. Large eggplants benefit from salting to extract their juices—small eggplants are less bitter, and can often be cooked without salting.

Yellow Curry

Potatoes are not highly regarded in Thai cooking because rice is the traditional staple food, but this dish is a tasty exception.

serves 4

2 garlic cloves, finely chopped

1¼-inch/3-cm piece galangal, finely chopped

1 lemongrass stalk, finely chopped

1 tsp coriander seeds

3 tbsp vegetable oil

2 tsp Thai red curry paste

½ tsp ground turmeric

scant 1 cup coconut milk

9 oz/250 g potatoes, cut into cubes

generous ⅓ cup vegetable stock

4⅜ cups fresh young spinach leaves

1 small onion, thinly sliced into rings

Method

❶ Place the garlic, galangal, lemongrass, and coriander seeds in a mortar and then crush with a pestle to make a smooth paste.

❷ Heat 2 tablespoons of the oil in a large, heavy-bottom skillet or preheated wok. Stir in the fresh garlic and spice paste and stir-fry over high heat for 30 seconds. Stir in the curry paste and turmeric, add the coconut milk, and bring to a boil.

❸ Add the potatoes and stock. Return to a boil, then reduce the heat and let simmer, uncovered, for 10–12 minutes, or until the potatoes are almost tender.

❹ Stir in the spinach and let simmer until the leaves have wilted.

❺ Heat the remaining oil in a separate skillet, add the onion, and cook until crisp and golden brown. Place on top of the curry just before serving.

Cook's tip

Choose a firm, waxy potato for this dish, one that will keep its shape during cooking, in preference to a mealy variety that will break up easily.

Greek Beans

This dish contains many typical Greek flavors, such as lemon and garlic, for a really flavorsome recipe. The fresh oregano and black olives give it a real taste of the Mediterranean.

serves 4

14 oz/400 g canned Great Northern beans, drained and rinsed

1 tbsp olive oil

3 garlic cloves, crushed

scant 2 cups vegetable stock

1 bay leaf

2 fresh oregano sprigs

1 tbsp tomato paste

juice of 1 lemon

1 small red onion, chopped

1 heaping tbsp pitted black olives, halved

salt and pepper

Method

❶ Place the Great Northern beans in an ovenproof casserole dish, add the oil and crushed garlic, and cook over low heat, stirring occasionally, for 4–5 minutes.

❷ Add the stock, bay leaf, oregano, tomato paste, lemon juice, and red onion and stir to mix. Cover and let simmer for 1 hour, or until the sauce has thickened.

❸ Stir in the black olives, then season the beans to taste. This dish is delicious served either warm or cold.

Cook's tip

You can substitute other canned beans for the Great Northern beans—try cannellini or black-eye peas or chickpeas. Drain and rinse them before use—canned beans often have sugar or salt added.

Spiced Cashew Curry

This unusual vegetarian dish is best served as a side dish with other curries and with rice to soak up the wonderfully rich, spiced juices.

serves 4

generous 1⅝ cups unsalted cashews

1 small fresh green chile, seeded and chopped

1 tsp coriander seeds

1 tsp cumin seeds

2 cardamom pods, crushed

1 tbsp corn oil

1 onion, thinly sliced

1 garlic clove, crushed

1 cinnamon stick

½ tsp ground turmeric

4 tbsp coconut cream

1¼ cups hot vegetable stock

3 kaffir lime leaves, finely shredded

freshly cooked jasmine rice, to serve

Method

❶ Soak the cashews in cold water for 8 hours, or overnight, then drain well. Place the coriander seeds, cumin seeds, and cardamom pods into a mortar and crush with a pestle.

❷ Heat the oil in a heavy-bottom skillet and stir-fry the onion and garlic over medium heat for 2–3 minutes to soften, but not brown. Add the chile, crushed spices, cinnamon stick, and turmeric and stir-fry for an additional 1 minute.

❸ Add the coconut cream and the hot stock to the skillet. Bring to a boil, then add the cashews and lime leaves. Reduce the heat, cover, and let simmer for 20 minutes. Serve hot, accompanied by freshly cooked jasmine rice.

Cook's tip

All spices give the best flavor when freshly crushed, but if you prefer, you can use ground spices instead of putting them into a mortar and crushing with a pestle.

Desserts

Creamed Rice Pudding

This rich, creamy rice dessert is a really comforting treat on cold winter days.
You can serve it with a helping of canned or stewed fruit, or just enjoy it on its own.

serves 4

⅔ cup short-grain rice

4 cups milk

generous ½ cup sugar

1 tsp vanilla extract

To decorate

ground cinnamon

cinnamon sticks

Method

❶ Rinse the rice well under cold running water and drain. Pour the milk into a large, heavy-bottom pan, add the sugar, and bring to a boil, stirring.

❷ Add the rice to the pan, then reduce the heat, cover, and let simmer gently, stirring occasionally, for 1 hour, or until the milk has been absorbed.

❸ Stir in the vanilla extract. Transfer to tall heatproof glasses, lightly dust with ground cinnamon, and serve at once, decorated with cinnamon sticks.

Variation

For an orange flavor, omit the sugar and vanilla and stir 3 tablespoons of honey and the finely grated rind of 1 orange into the milk in Step 1.

Teacup Pudding

This is such an easy dessert to make, because all the ingredients, except the allspice, can be measured in the same cup. It tastes best served with a generous helping of warmed custard.

serves 4

butter, for greasing
1 cup self-rising flour
1 tsp allspice
1 cup brown sugar

1 cup shredded shortening
1 cup currants
1 cup milk
custard, to serve

Method

❶ Grease a 4-cup ovenproof bowl with butter. Sift the flour and allspice into a mixing bowl and stir in the sugar, shortening, and currants, then add the milk and mix well. Spoon the mixture into the prepared bowl.

❷ Cut out a circle of waxed paper and a circle of foil 3 inches/7.5 cm larger than the rim of the ovenproof bowl. Place the paper circle on top of the foil circle, grease it, and pleat both circles across the center. Place them over the bowl, paper-side down, and tie round the rim with string.

❸ Place the ovenproof bowl on a trivet in a large pan and fill with boiling water to come halfway up the sides. Alternatively, place it in a steamer over a pan of boiling water. Let steam for 3 hours, then carefully remove from the pan. Discard the covering, turn out onto a warmed serving dish, and serve with custard.

Cook's tip

It doesn't matter whether you use a standard measuring cup or an ordinary teacup to measure the ingredients, because the proportions remain the same.

Clafoutis

Although the many different recipes for this unusual, batter-based dessert may use a variety of fruits, cherries are the classic filling in Limousin in France, where the dish originated.

serves 4

1 lb/450 g sweet black cherries

2 tbsp cherry brandy

1 tbsp confectioners' sugar, plus extra for dusting

butter, for greasing

Batter

3 tbsp all-purpose flour

3 tbsp sugar

¾ cup light cream

2 eggs, lightly beaten

grated rind of ½ lemon

¼ tsp vanilla extract

Method

❶ Preheat the oven to 375°F/190°C. Pit the cherries, then place in a bowl with the cherry brandy and confectioners' sugar and mix together. Cover with plastic wrap and let stand for 1 hour.

❷ Meanwhile, grease a shallow, ovenproof dish with butter. To make the batter, sift the flour into a bowl and stir in the sugar. Gradually whisk in the light cream, beaten eggs, lemon rind, and vanilla extract. Whisk constantly until the batter is completely smooth.

❸ Spoon the cherries into the ovenproof dish and pour the batter over them to cover. Bake in the preheated oven for 45 minutes, or until golden and set. Lightly dust with extra confectioners' sugar and serve warm, or let cool to room temperature before serving.

Cook's tip

Traditionally, in Limousin, the cherries are not pitted before cooking, because the pits are thought to release extra flavor into the dessert.

Tarte Tatin

This upside-down apple tart has been a speciality of Sologne in the Loire valley for centuries, but was made famous by the Tatin sisters who ran a hotel-restaurant in Lamotte-Beuvron at the beginning of the twentieth century.

serves 8

8 oz/225 g basic pie dough, thawed if frozen

all-purpose flour, for dusting

10 eating apples, such as Golden Delicious

4 tbsp lemon juice

4 oz/115 g unsalted butter, diced

generous ½ cup superfine sugar

½ tsp ground cinnamon

Method

❶ Preheat the oven to 450°F/230°C. Roll out the pie dough on a lightly floured counter into a ¼-inch/5-mm thick circle, about 11 inches/28 cm in diameter. Transfer to a lightly floured baking sheet and let chill in the refrigerator for 30 minutes.

❷ Peel, halve, and core the apples, then brush with the lemon juice to prevent any discoloration. Heat the butter, sugar, and cinnamon in a 10-inch/25-cm tarte tatin pan, or heavy-bottom skillet with an ovenproof handle, over low heat, stirring occasionally, until the butter has melted and the sugar has dissolved. Cook for an additional 6–8 minutes, or until the mixture is a light caramel color. Remove from the heat.

❸ Arrange the apples in the pan or skillet, packing them in tightly. Return to the heat and cook for 25 minutes, or until the apples are tender and lightly colored. Remove from the heat and let cool slightly.

❹ Place the dough over the apples, tucking in the edges. Prick the top and bake in the preheated oven for 30 minutes, or until golden. Let cool slightly, then run a knife around the edge of the pan to loosen the pastry. Invert onto a plate and serve warm.

Cook's tip

To achieve the best decorative effect when the tart is turned over, pack the halved apples in the pan with their cut sides facing up in Step 3.

Flambéed Peaches

This dessert is a fabulous end to a dinner party—especially if your guests are watching you cook. It makes a luxurious but, at the same time, refreshing final course.

serves 4

3 tbsp unsalted butter

3 tbsp brown sugar

4 tbsp orange juice

4 peaches, peeled, halved, and pitted

2 tbsp almond liqueur or peach brandy

4 tbsp toasted slivered almonds

Method

❶ Heat the butter, brown sugar, and orange juice in a large, heavy-bottom skillet over low heat, stirring constantly, until the butter has melted and the sugar has dissolved.

❷ Add the peaches and cook for 1–2 minutes on each side, or until golden.

❸ Add the almond liqueur and ignite with a match or taper. When the flames have died down, transfer to serving dishes, sprinkle with toasted slivered almonds, and serve at once.

Cook's tip

Igniting the spirit will burn off the alcohol and mellow the flavor. However, if you are serving this dessert to children, you can omit the almond liqueur or brandy.

Apple Fritters

This is a very popular choice for family meals, as children and adults alike love the flavor and crispy texture of the apple rings—and you don't need a spoon or fork to eat them.

serves 4

scant ¾ cup all-purpose flour

pinch of salt

2 egg yolks

1 egg white

1 tbsp corn oil

⅔ cup milk

1 lb/450 g cooking apples

juice of 1 lemon

superfine sugar, for sprinkling

4 oz/115 g unsalted butter

sour cream, to serve

Method

❶ Sift the flour and salt into a mixing bowl. Make a well in the center and add the egg yolks, egg white, and oil. Gradually incorporate the flour into the liquid with a wooden spoon. Gradually beat in the milk and continue beating to make a smooth batter. Cover with plastic wrap and let stand for 30 minutes.

❷ Peel and core the apples, then cut them into rings about ¼-inch/5-mm thick. Spread them out on a plate and then sprinkle with the lemon juice and superfine sugar.

❸ Melt the butter in a large, heavy-bottom skillet over medium heat. Dip the apple rings into the batter, one at a time, then drop them into the skillet. Cook for 2–3 minutes on each side, or until golden. Transfer to a serving platter, sprinkle with more superfine sugar, and serve with sour cream.

Cook's tip

Choose firm, tart apples for this dish, such as Granny Smiths. Once they are cut, they should be sprinkled with lemon juice immediately and cooked quickly to prevent any discoloration.

Syllabub

Wine, brandy, and cream make this old-fashioned dessert wonderfully self-indulgent—and it is guaranteed to make an impression if you serve it at a dinner party.

serves 6

¾ cup Madeira

2 tbsp brandy

grated rind of 1 lemon

½ cup lemon juice

generous ½ cup superfine sugar

2½ cups heavy cream

10 amaretti cookies or

ratafias, crumbled

ground cinnamon, to dust

lemon slices, to decorate

Method

❶ Whisk the Madeira, brandy, lemon rind, lemon juice, and superfine sugar in a bowl until combined.

❷ Add the cream to the bowl and continue whisking until the mixture is thick in consistency.

❸ Divide the cookies between 6 long-stemmed glasses or sundae dishes. Fill each glass or dish with the syllabub mixture and let chill in the refrigerator until ready to serve, if desired. Dust the surface of each dessert with ground cinnamon and decorate with lemon slices, and serve.

Cook's tip

Madeira is a fortified wine from the island of the same name. It may be dry, medium, or sweet. Dessert Madeira is best for this recipe— use Bual or Malmsey.

Zabaglione

This light and frothy, warm dessert, which originates from Italy, is a welcome treat at the end of a meal. You should serve it as soon as it is ready, to appreciate its full flavor.

serves 6

4 egg yolks

generous ⅓ cup superfine sugar

½ cup Marsala wine

amaretti cookies, to serve

Method

❶ Half fill a pan with water and bring to a boil. Reduce the heat so that the water is barely simmering. Beat the egg yolks and sugar in a heatproof bowl with an electric whisk until pale and creamy.

❷ Set the bowl over the pan of water. Do not let the base touch the surface of the water, or the egg yolks will scramble.

❸ Gradually add the Marsala wine, beating constantly with the electric whisk. Continue beating until the mixture is thick and has increased in volume. Pour into heatproof glasses or bowls and serve at once with amaretti cookies.

Cook's tip

Decorate the zabaglione with a slit strawberry, placed on the rim of the glass, or serve with ladyfingers or crisp cookies.

Recipe List

- Apple Fritters *90* • Bacon & Lentil Soup *12* • Beef & Vegetable Soup *14*

- Beef in Beer with Herb Dumplings *18* • Beef Stroganoff *16*

- Bell Pepper & Mushroom Hash *60* • Boston Fish Pie *52* • Brunswick Stew *32*

- Cauliflower Bake *58* • Chicken Pasanda *36* • Clafoutis *84* •

- Cock-a-Leekie *10* • Coq au Vin *38* • Corn, Potato & Cheese Soup *56*

- Creamed Rice Pudding *80* • Flambéed Peaches *88* • French Country Casserole *26*

- Greek Beans *74* • Irish Stew *22* • Italian Turkey Steaks *42* • Jambalaya *34*

- Mexican Turkey *40* • Moroccan Lamb *24* • Moules Marinières *50*

- Paella del Mar *48* • Paprika Pork *28* • Pot-Roast Pork *30*

- Potato-Topped Vegetables *64* • Risotto Primavera *66* • Seafood Risotto *44*

- Spiced Cashew Curry *76* • Stifado *20* • Sweet & Sour Vegetables *70*

- Syllabub *92* • Tarte Tatin *86* • Teacup Pudding *82* • Thai Shrimp Curry *46*

- Vegetable Chili *68* • Winter Cobbler *62* • Yellow Curry *72* • Zabaglione *94*